The Joy of Being

By the same author

THE GRAND DESIGN
Volumes I - V

THE GRAND DESIGN
Selected Excerpts

A FREE SPIRIT
Dialogue with Margaret Anna Cusack,
the Nun of Kenmare

LIVING WITHOUT FEAR
Dialogue with J. Krishnamurti

The Joy of Being

By

Patrick Francis

Illustrations by Michel

Auricle Enterprises

Copyright © 2002 by Patrick Francis

First published 2002

Auricle Enterprises
30 Old Court Manor
Firhouse
Dublin 24
Tel (01) 452 3793

All rights reserved. Other than for review purposes, no part of this book may be reproduced, stored in a retrieval system or transmitted in any form or by any means, electronic, photocopying, recording, video recording, or otherwise, without prior permission in writing from the publisher.

ISBN 0 9525509 8 9
Typesetting by John Lundberg
Printed by ColourBooks Ltd., Baldoyle, Dublin 13, Ireland

INTRODUCTION

During the period 1981-1996 I wrote and published five books, entitled *The Grand Design I - V*, in collaboration with a spirit being known to me as Shebaka. The books were subsequently published in two volumes in 2000 by Hampton Roads Publishing Company in America.

To date, Volume I has been translated into German and Spanish (an expanded edition) and published in Germany and Mexico, respectively.

This book represents a new development for me in that, while the text consists of excerpts from *The Grand Design* series, each page is faced by a related illustration. In all my communication with Shebaka I have been conscious of his ever-bubbling sense of humour and his gentle reminders that we humans tend to take ourselves too seriously. I think that Michel's illustrations have wonderfully captured the spirit, including the profundity and yet the simplicity, of Shebaka's teachings.

Born in France and educated in both France and America, Michel has drawn ever since he could hold a pencil. He is also very active in the fields of photography, writing and international publishing.

Patrick Francis
(Paddy McMahon)
November 2002

Shebaka

I have let myself be called Shebaka because I knew the sound of the name would have a certain appeal to you. I am coming to talk to you from a vibration where names are no longer important, where indeed communication is instantaneous and so open that one communicates simply by being. Thus there is never any misunderstanding. I retain a memory of the circumstances of Earth and I know the constraints that they put on communication.

The Joy of Being

The essence of spirituality is enjoyment.

It is a celebration of the joy of being.

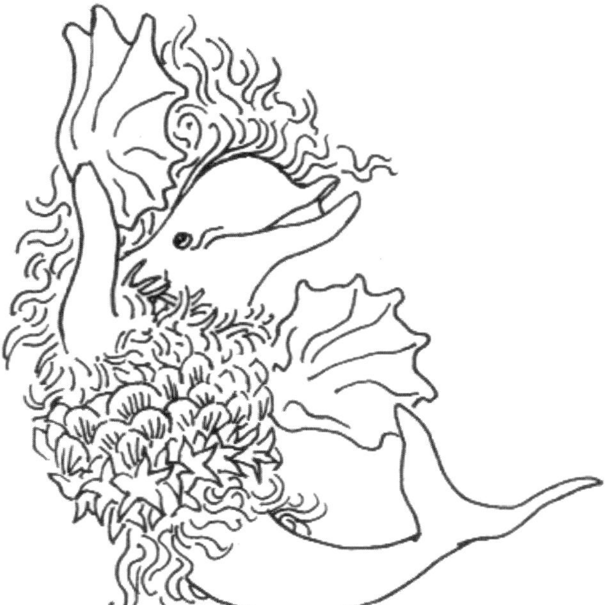

The Nature of Being

Take a rose, for instance. Nothing could be simpler and nothing is more beautiful. The nature of being is as the rose. It is an unfolding of love. The bud symbolises the soul as yet unaware of its own beauty and magnitude. Then the blooming comes as light flows and represents the slow awakening of the soul to its destiny.

cor! Look at that

God

God is love, infinite love.
In saying that, I mean that God
is the animating force
in all expression,
which includes all life
and all activities of life.

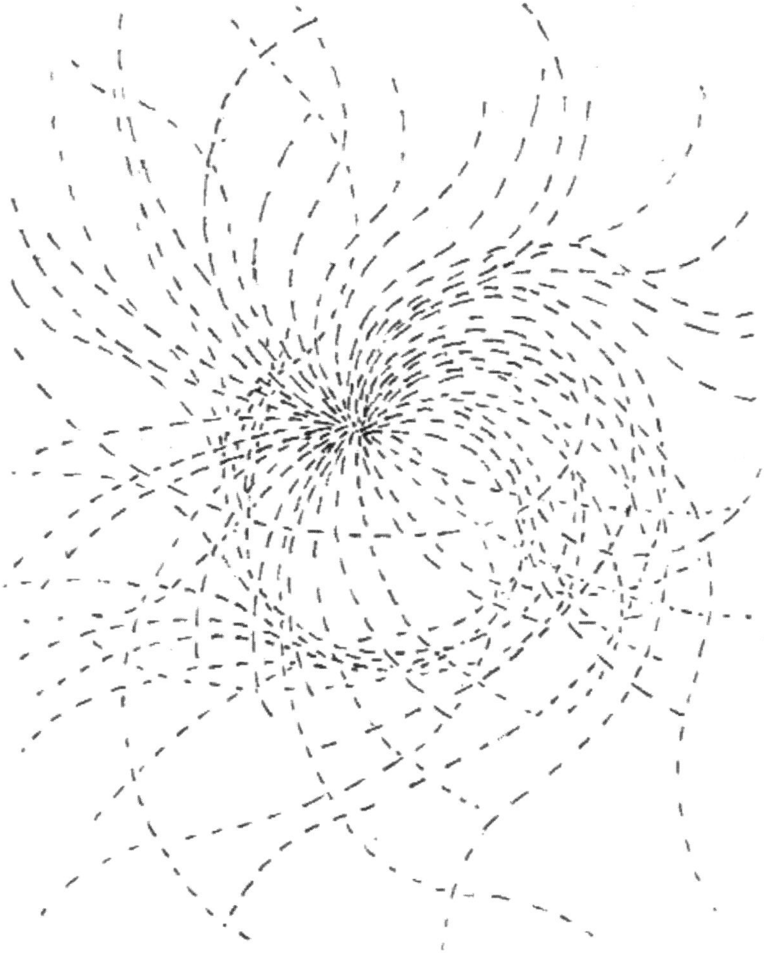

Soul

Each soul is an infinite part of God.
The God within us is the supply of energy that animates us.
It is an unfailing, unending source of supply, no matter what transitional forms our evolutionary journeys involve.
The love that is God does not have to express itself in any particular pattern; it evolves in whatever way it wishes.

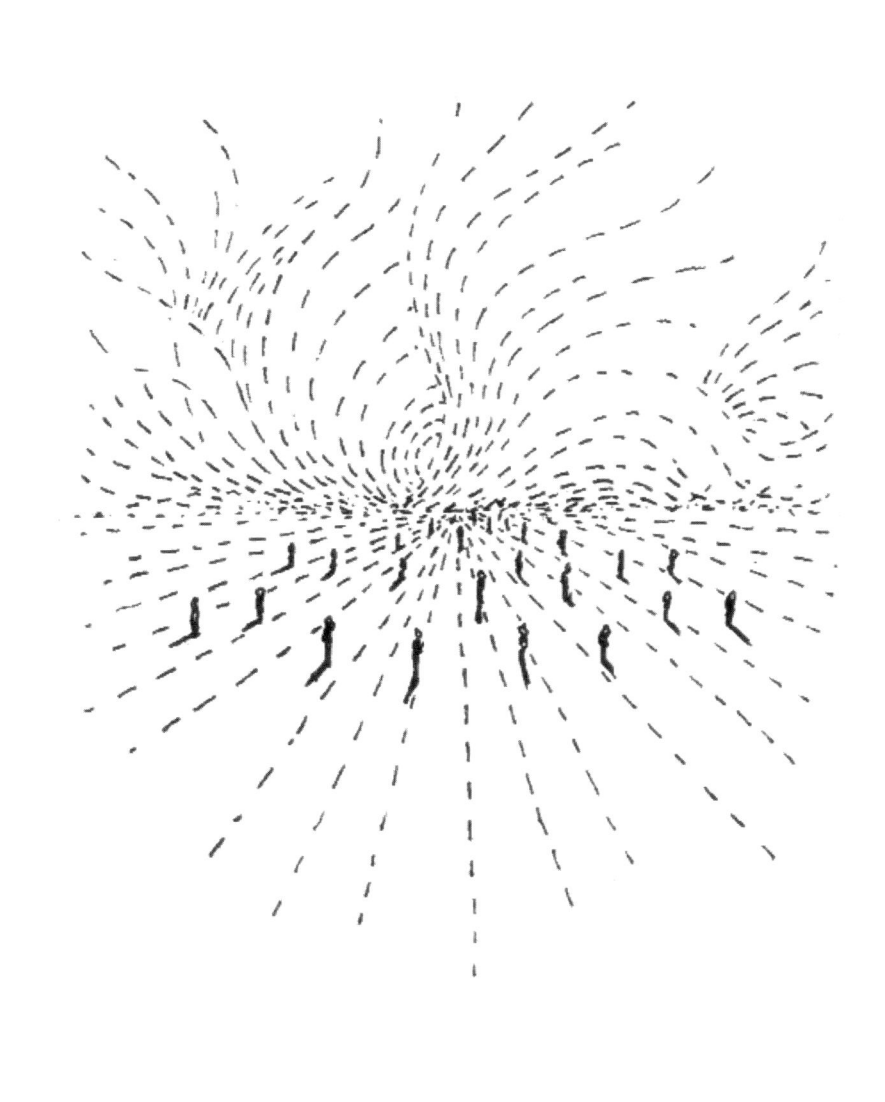

Truth

There is only one truth - God. There is only one true God. These are the sort of factual statements which, without elaboration, contribute to the spread of ignorance because of people's tendencies towards confining God within the structures of rigid beliefs. However, when it's accepted that God is all and nothing exists outside of God, it can be seen that there's an infinity of truths in God. For example, each soul is uniquely an expression of God.

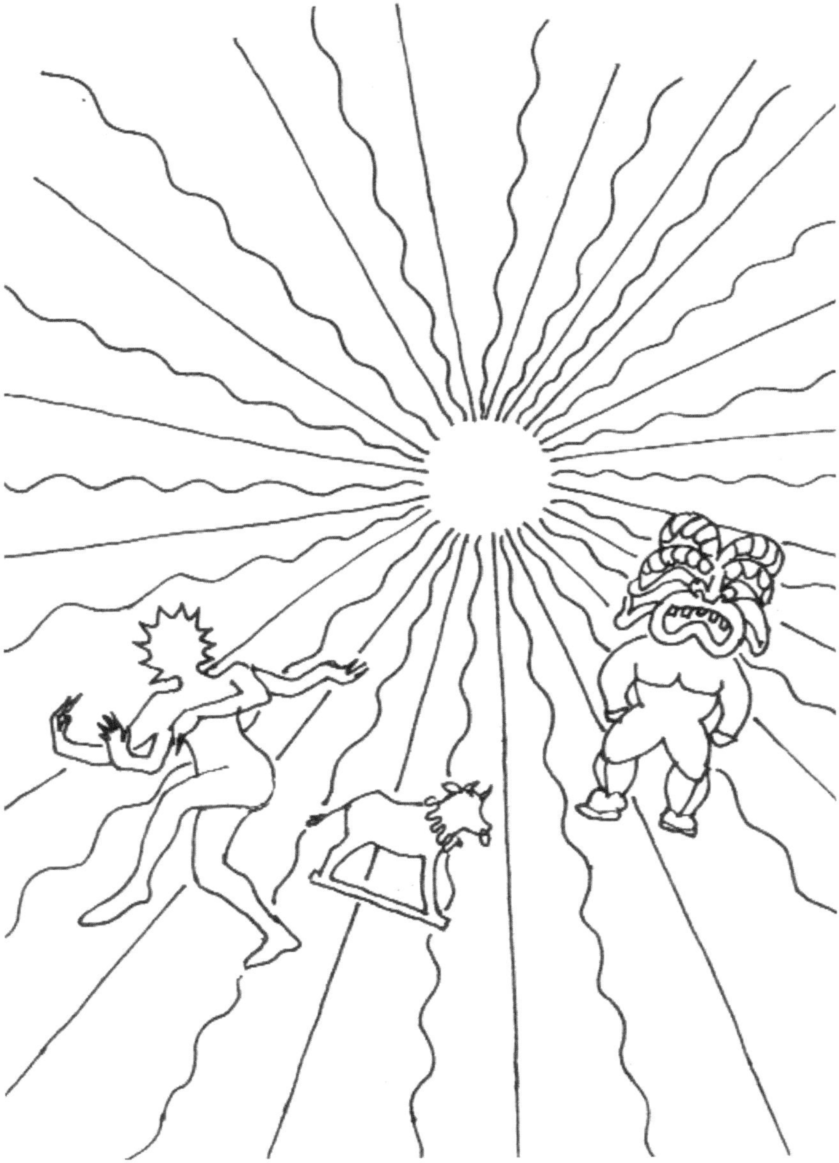

Guardian Angels

People are being reintroduced to the idea that they have guardian angels, something which many believed and believe as children. These angels are evolved souls who are familiar with Earth's conditions and have already learned the lessons it has to offer. The soul has free will to decide whether it wants an angel (guide) to help it. The choice is made before the soul's entry or re-entry to Earth.

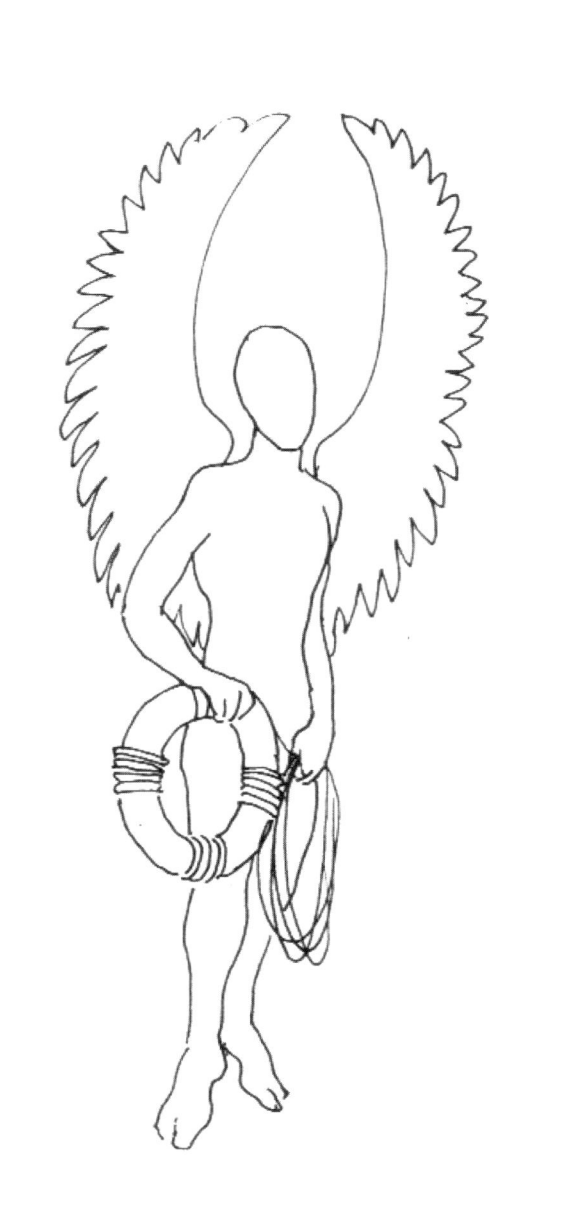

Help

There has never been, nor is there now, any person on Earth, no matter how evolved, who did not, or does not, need help. Each person begins life as a child, with total dependence for survival on another or others; and all through his/her life on Earth that person has to be helped in different ways by many people. It stands to reason that if people need so much help with the physical aspects of life, they also need help with the non-physical aspects. Guides (guardian angels) are there to help with all aspects of life.

Reincarnation

There is no more mystery about the fact of reincarnation than there is about rosebushes repeating the growth of roses.

The purpose of reincarnation is, of course, to give souls repeated opportunities to raise their awareness. Earth provides a wide range of such opportunities.

Free Will

Expression evolved out of God into individual parts. Each part retained the full freedom of spirit which it always had. There was no such thing as reporting back to some superior being looking for permission to do this or that or the other; it was completely free to express itself in any way it chose. This is still the position and will always continue to be so; it cannot be otherwise.

Life on Earth

Everything on Earth is infused with love; for instance, grass, water; but such things aren't souls. They evolved in the Earth scene to help sustain life in physical form. Life on Earth can be categorised into two forms, stationary - in the sense of not capable of moving around - and non-stationary. Stationary life includes plants, trees, grass, flowers. Non-stationary life includes birds, insects, fish, animals, human beings. Stationary life is not soul. Non-stationary life is.

"I'M AFRAID I'M NOT A SOUL. TRY MY FRIEND OVER THERE"

Why human?

One of the reasons why souls can gain considerable benefit from adopting human form is that they have allowed themselves to become limited by structured thinking, and by coming into that type of environment they are, ideally, brought up against the effects of such thinking; whereas in spirit, because vibrations don't mix in the same way as they do on Earth (in spirit like tends to associate exclusively with like), they might continue to exist indefinitely within an unchanging framework of thought.

BODY FITTING

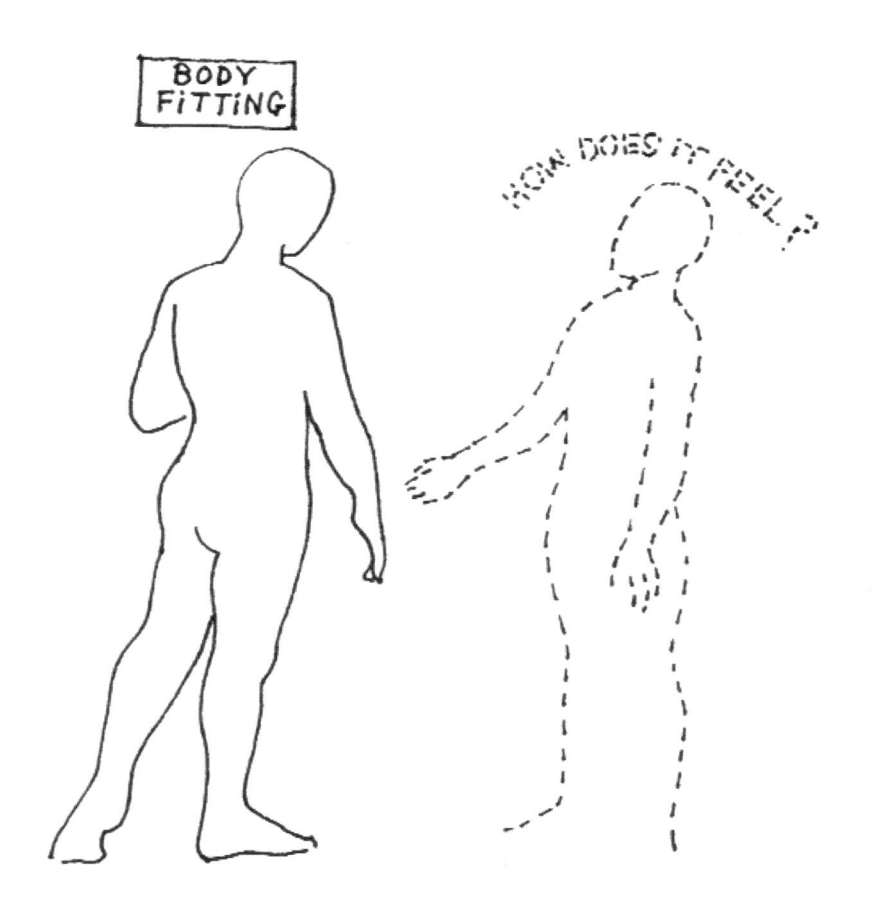

HOW DOES IT FEEL?

Inequalities

Inequalities in the human scene are highlighted by the vast differences in the conditions under which people are born and live. Some people are physically frail and seem to have no resistance to infections; others are robust and immune to physical illness. Many are born with deformities; others don't have any physical defects. It would, I suggest, be impossible to explain in any reasonable way how there could be any meaning to life in the face of its inequalities if there were no continuity of life.

Reality

How do you create your reality?
Through your feelings and
thoughts. All creation originates
in the mind (soul) of its creator;
nothing is built in
the external, physical world
unless it is first designed
in somebody's mind. All
souls create their own individual
universes - their own reality.

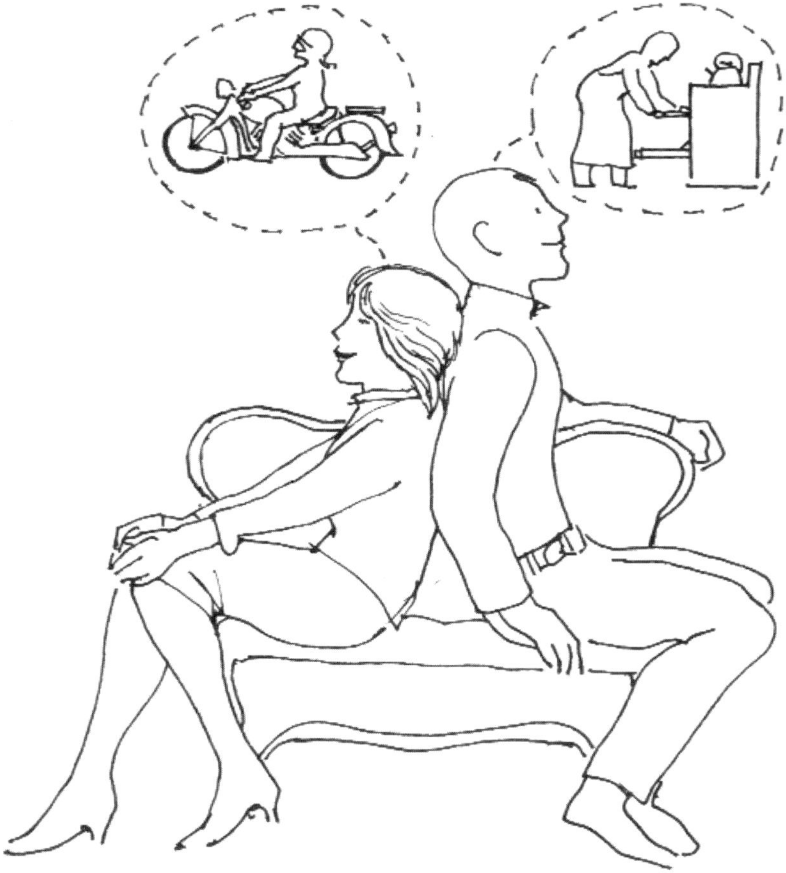

Soul Expression

If one accepts that there's life after death, what continues?
Not the physical body, obviously, nor any material possessions.
The soul continues.
What constitutes the soul?
Feelings and thoughts - the reality that's created within each person.
All that people take with them when their life on Earth ceases is their state of being.

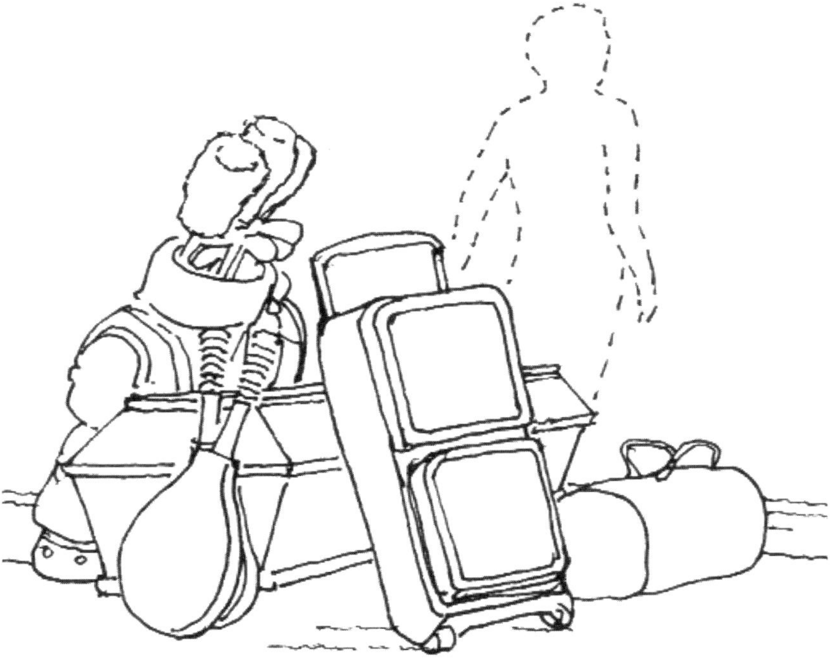

Transition

The best condition of all in which to make the transition to life in spirit is one of complete acceptance of the continuity of life, of individual responsibility for spiritual development and of the fact that there are many evolved souls only waiting to be asked for help. A soul leaving its body in that frame of mind will make rapid progress through the stages back to full awareness.

Partings

It is a feature of life on Earth that it's full of partings, in a physical sense, of one kind or another, the most notable being the death of the body.
It's a great comfort to people if they can accept that these partings are not real; one soul is never more than a thought away from another.

Choices

The soul performs actions which bring consequences. In order to make progress along the path of awareness it is faced with choices, including the possibility of reincarnation.

Each individual chooses its own physical habitat and lifestyle for a particular purpose. The purpose in most cases is ultimately growth in awareness.

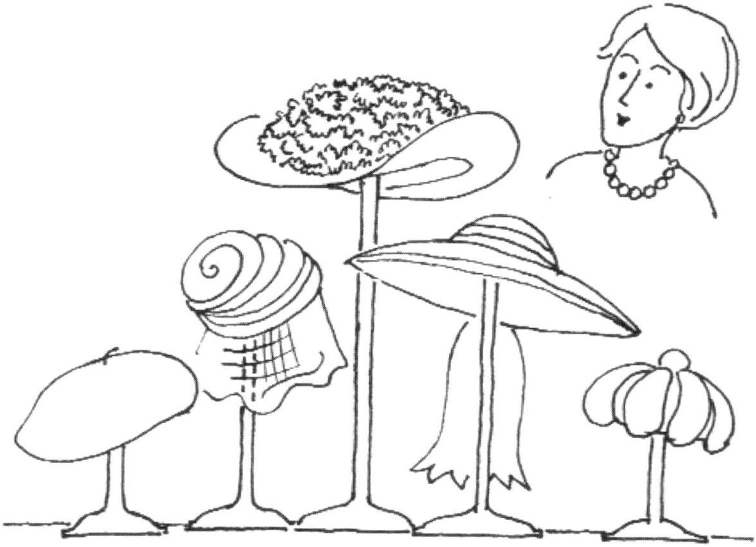

Illness

It is believed by some that if the soul is in tune with its life purpose the body should not succumb to illness. This is a misunderstanding of the whole design of Earth existence, which is to present people with learning experiences in order to help them to increase their awareness.

Illness or disability can be a most valuable learning experience. So can healing or being healed.

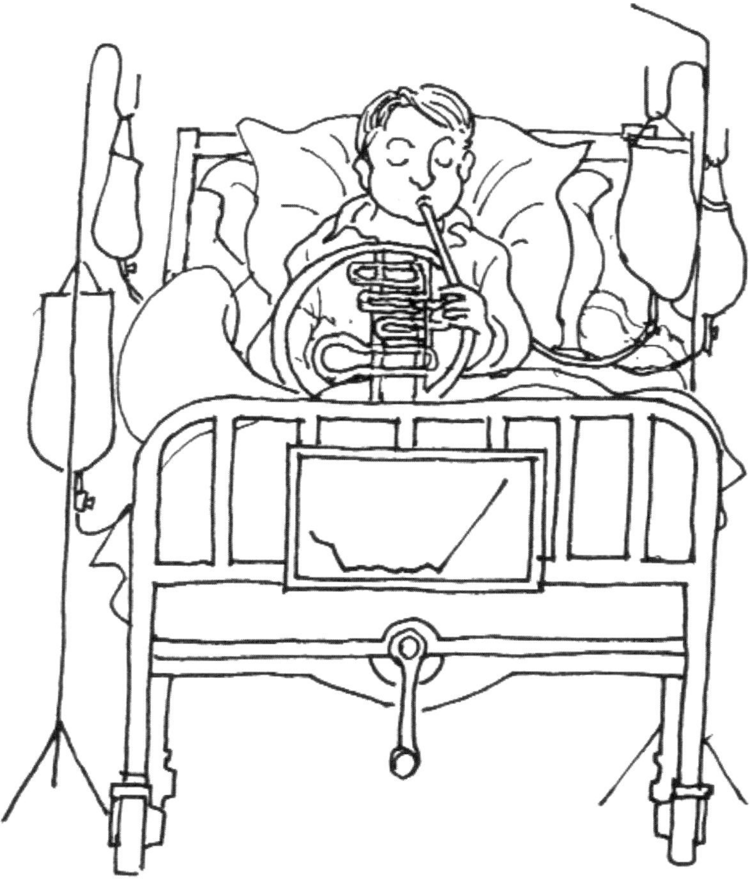

Predictions

Souls in spirit are often not any wiser or more advanced than souls temporarily on Earth but they are in a better position to see the overall picture of happenings on Earth and therefore to make more accurate predictions. The more aware a soul is the less likely it is to make predictions if there is any risk that they may influence the exercise of free will; however, if that risk isn't present it will probably enjoy chancing its arm.

Perfection

Perfection is a word which implies a state where everything stops - no going beyond it. In the ultimate state of awareness there's no such thing as perfection in that sense - which would be very boring anyway, just stagnation; rather it is a state of continually evolving consciousness. So the perfection that each soul will show as it sheds its unawareness will not be dull, or boring, or stagnant. It will be without limitation of any kind.

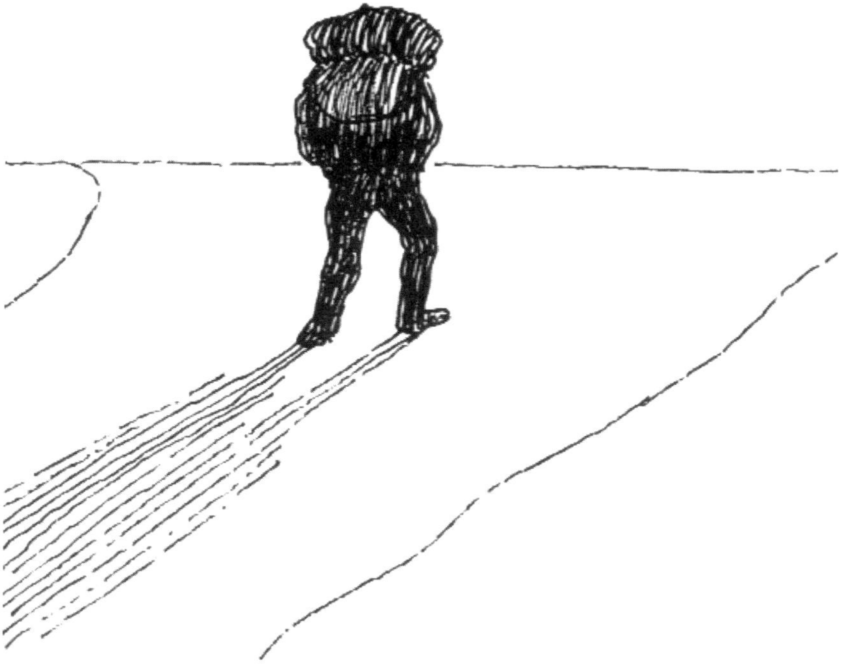

Unconditional Love

Unconditional love is unlimited acceptance of feeling in all its manifestations; in other words, whatever the expression is - tolerance, rejection, compassion, resentment, positive or negative - love accepts it as it is, without judgement.

In unconditionally loving acceptance of yourself it's impossible for you not to have respect for yourself and in such a way that it's impossible for anybody else to undermine that respect.

Violence : Peace

Violence in all its forms is an expression of inner conflict. When all people find peace in themselves there will be no violence. I'm optimistic because I can see how many people are looking, and beginning to look, within themselves. All through the evolution of the planet people have been looking to gods and gurus of one kind or another to tell them what to do. Now more and more people are accepting that the divine is within each of them and as they let it manifest they love themselves and others unconditionally.

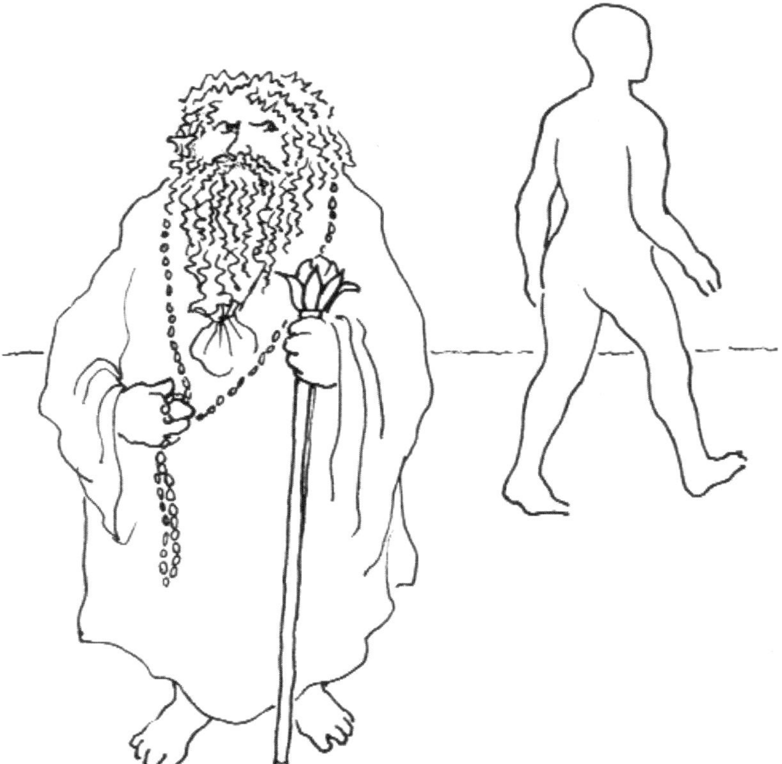

Education

It goes without saying that it's vitally important that children should be loved, and encouraged to express themselves freely. Educational systems should be organised, I suggest, in ways which would facilitate exploration and expression of each child's creative abilities. That would mean that there would be no set curricula, or, put another way, that there would be an unlimited range of curricula. Each child would get individual attention to a much greater extent than is possible at present.

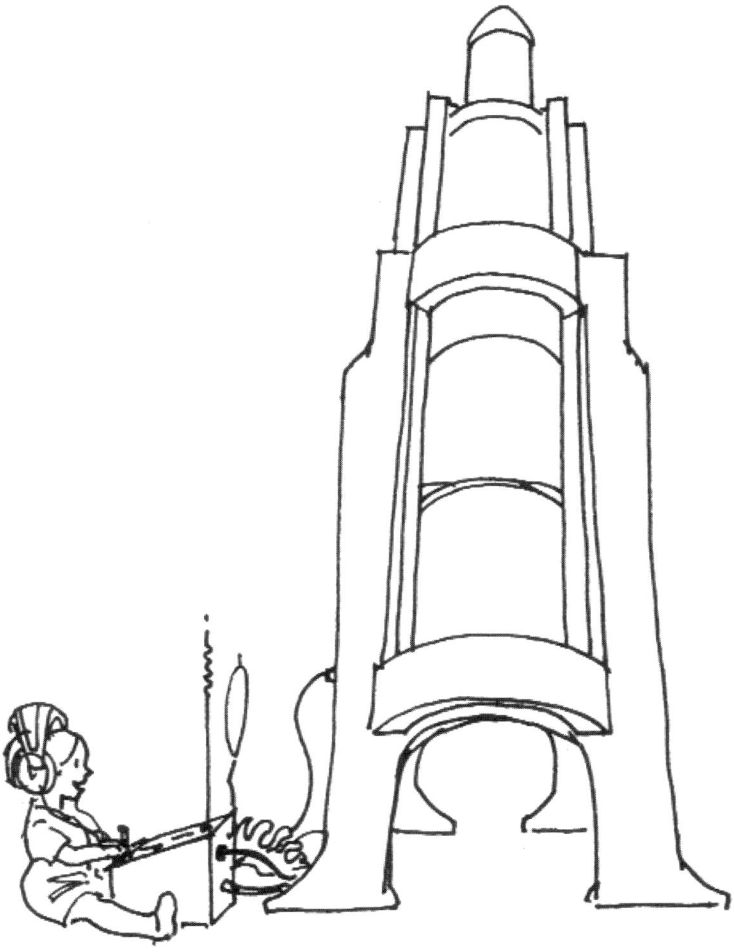

Prisons

Both prisoners and custodial staff are bound together in an enclosed cocoon of energy which is damaging for all of them.

It would be unhelpful and impractical for me to suggest something as radical as the closing down of all prisons immediately - although that's what I would do. People would probably be inclined to regard me as being too much under the influence of spirit(s) to be taken seriously!

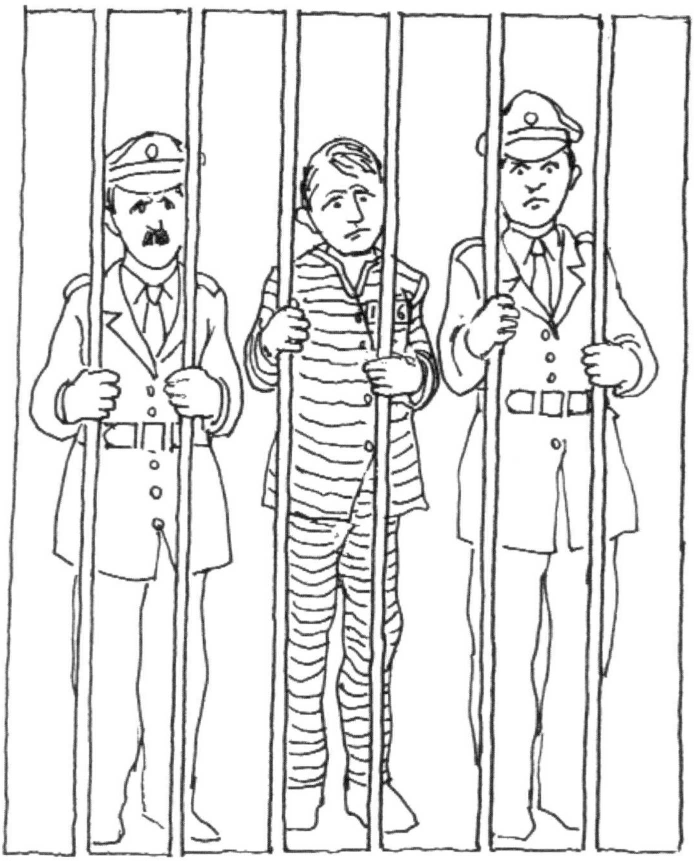

Ideal Living

Focusing on negativity, albeit with a positive aim, locks people into patterns of consciousness which affect how they relate to the world around them - which in turn influences what manifests for them in their day to day experiences. The ideal way to live, of course, is totally in the moment, free of the past and the future.

Experiences

As you exist in the present moment - and can only do so - the conglomeration of experiences which you have had in all your journeying are of no relevance or importance whatever except in so far as they continue to control your feelings and thoughts - in other words, how you carry the effects of them in yourself.

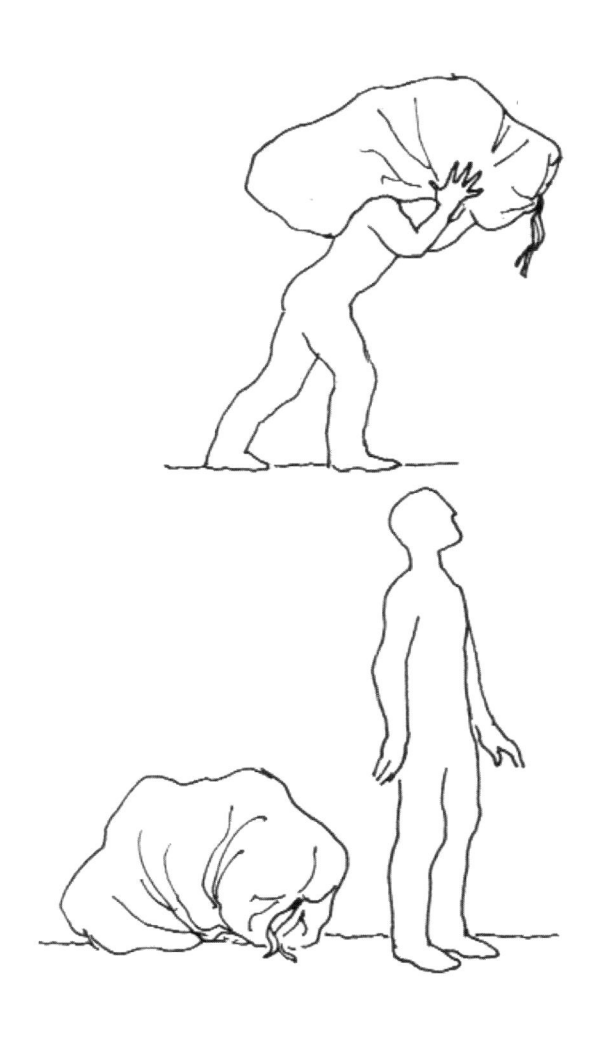

Evolution

Picture the soul as an electric light bulb which, though switched on, is buried in earth and doesn't show any light. When the earth is removed from it the bulb shows all its light. It's the same bulb all the time. That's the process of evolution in a nutshell. The light is the divinity which is always there even when it's hidden. What you call evil is the earth of unawareness which ultimately falls away and the divine reality is then revealed in all its glory.

Solutions

Humanity as a global concept takes its significance from the individuals who comprise it. As each individual finds inner completeness and peace the problems of humanity will be proportionately diminished. No revolution, no organisation, no religion, no system will provide adequate solutions, as should be obvious at this stage of evolution.. Global or generic answers could only be effective if people were to be standardised like robots.

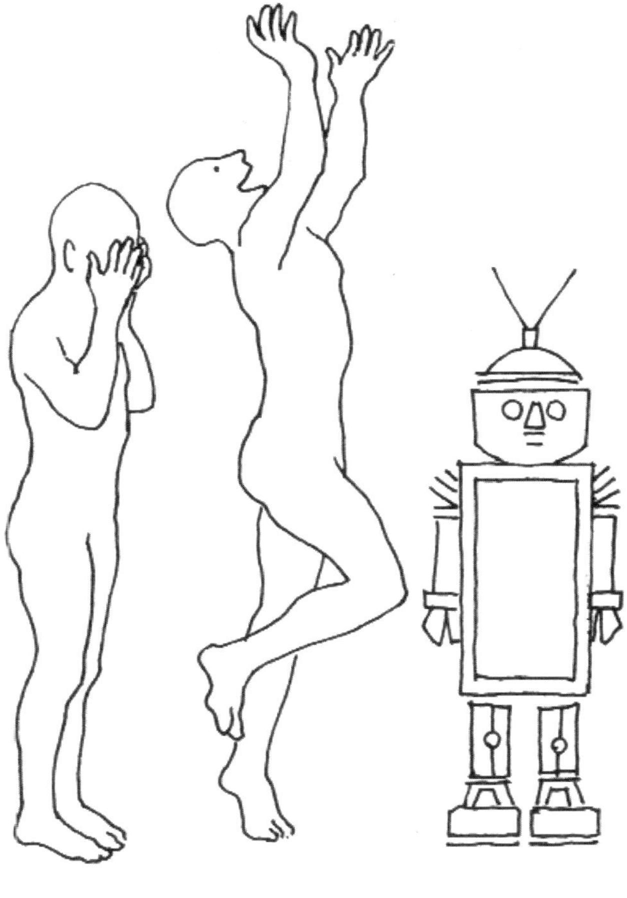

Cruelty to animals

Cruelty is a negation of soul to the extent that it obscures the loving nature of soul. There are obvious forms of cruelty such as torture, or what are known as blood sports, but there are many less obvious ones such as abandonment or neglect of dependent creatures.

Neither the hare which is pursued and mangled by dogs nor the dogs who do the pursuing and mangling are likely to be damaged to anything like the same extent as the organisers and participants in the event.

Animals and research

How about the use of animals for experimental research purposes in the interests of furthering scientific or medical knowledge?
I think that the best way I can answer that question is by asking another - how would you feel about a child being used in that way?

Conditioned thinking

Conditioned thinking has tended to isolate humanity into a prison of spirituality or spiritual growth being achieved through self-denial, self-sacrifice, suffering. Once that belief system is allowed to prevail, that's the only way that growth can occur.

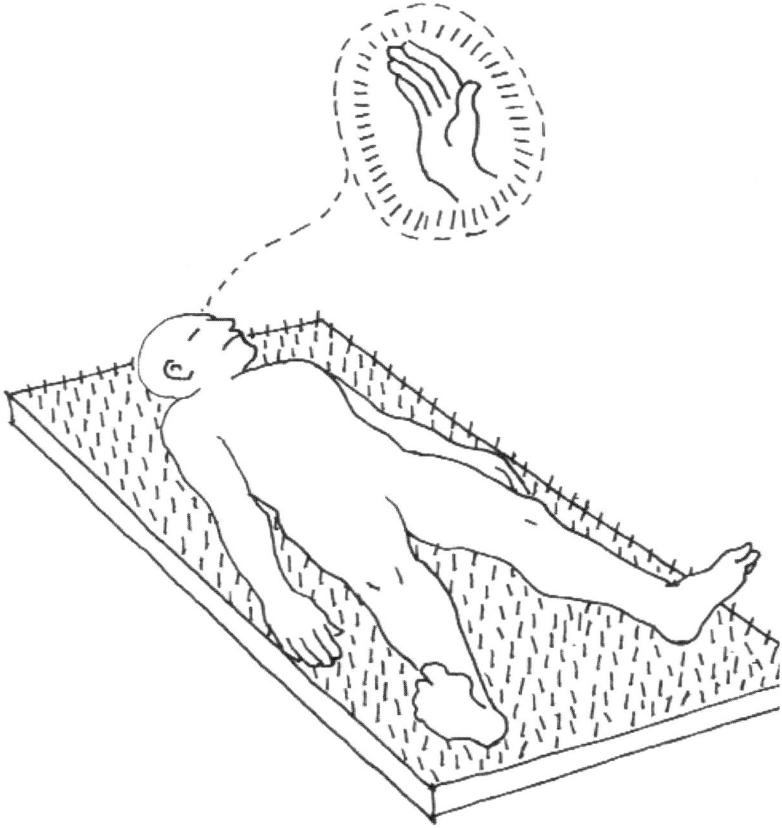

Another way

Love does not demand pain and suffering. Enjoyment is central to love. Life on Earth is intended to be an enjoyable experience. If that statement sounds in any way frivolous to you, please examine it. How do you enjoy yourself? Through self-expression, being how you like to be, doing what you like to do. And I'm sure you'll agree that ultimately your enjoyment comes from relating to people in the most loving possible ways.

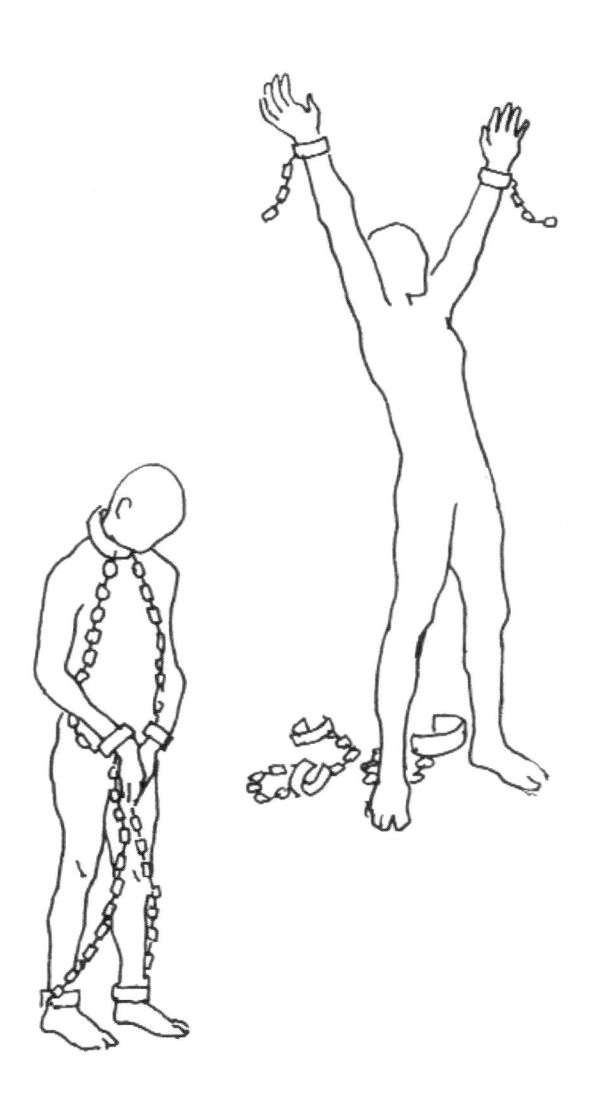

Gurus (self-styled)

Difficulties have arisen in human evolution when some people have set themselves up, or have been set up, as custodians of absolute truth and have dogmatically declared that the way to salvation is only possible through faithful adherence to that "truth". Sadly, such absolutism has attracted millions of devotees throughout human history and has led to all sorts of fanatical excesses. Any belief or practice which inhibits people's free will or seeks to control them within behavioural prescriptions is spiritually damaging.

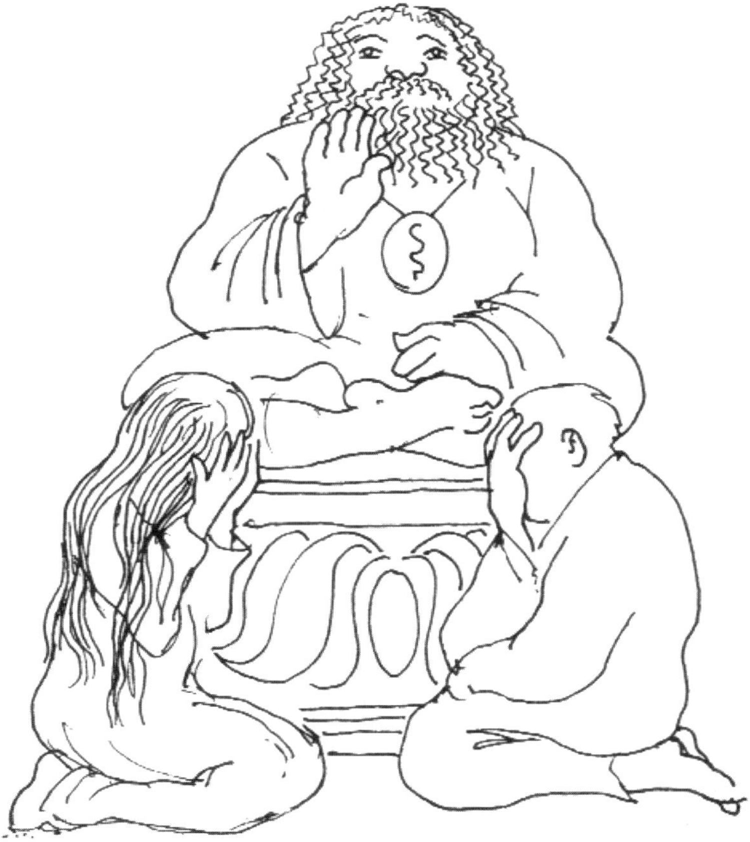

Your power

You have no idea of the power that's generated by the energy emanating from even one person; please don't undervalue how important your contribution is. It doesn't matter whether you're in a central position of obvious influence or in what may seem like an obscure backwater. When your starting point is finding peace within yourself and when you link with all the evolved loving energy of the universe the effect is astronomical.

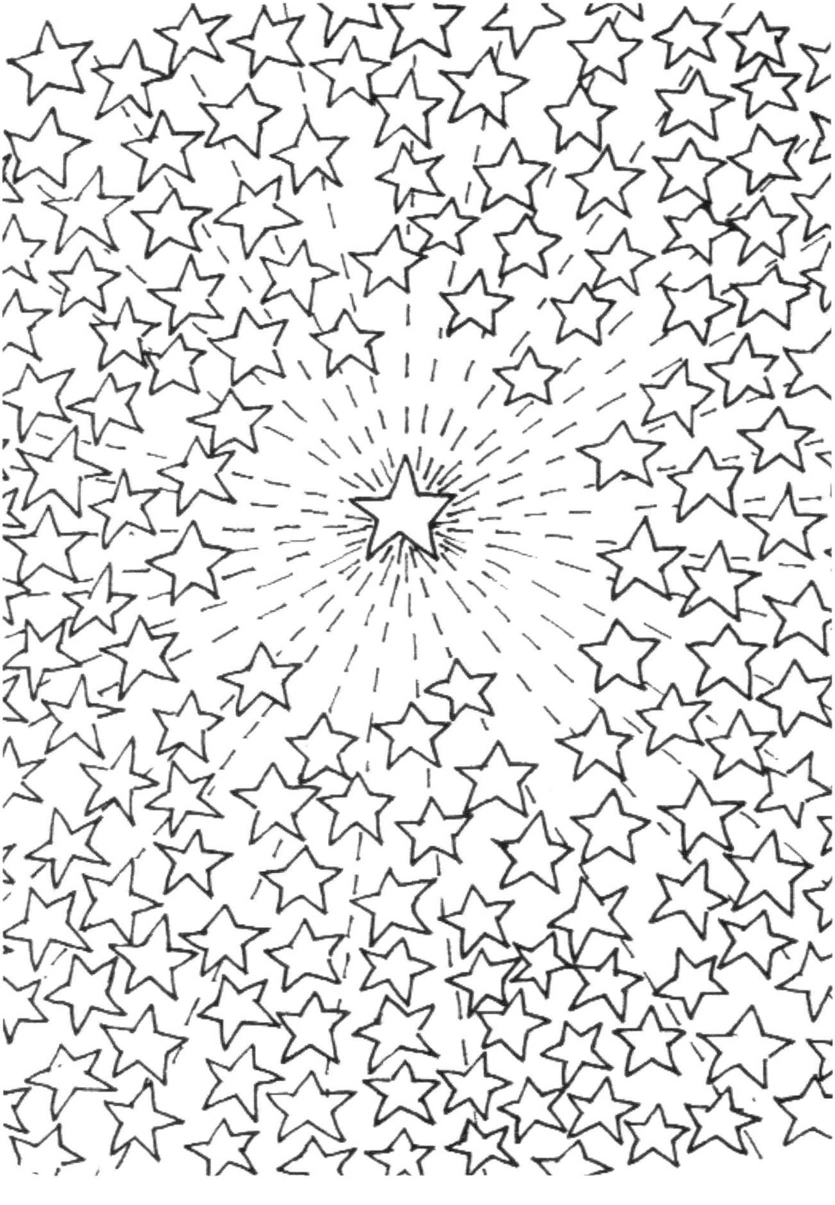

Special affinities

The expression of God into individual souls enabled special affinities between souls. The notion of God as an entity without a variety of individual expression is one of stagnation which is not consistent with evolving consciousness. The ultimate return to full awareness of souls still on that path will not result in a loss of individuality into a merging with a "Source". (There wouldn't be much fun in a soul communicating indefinitely with itself!)

No blame

A fundamental prerequisite for any soul seeking self-realisation, including, of course, taking full responsibility for itself, is that, ideally, it should never blame any other soul for whatever circumstances in which it may find itself. I don't mean articulating blame. I mean that no feeling involving blame exists. Paying lip service to the requirement, or accepting it intellectually only, is of no value spiritually; it's the feeling that matters.

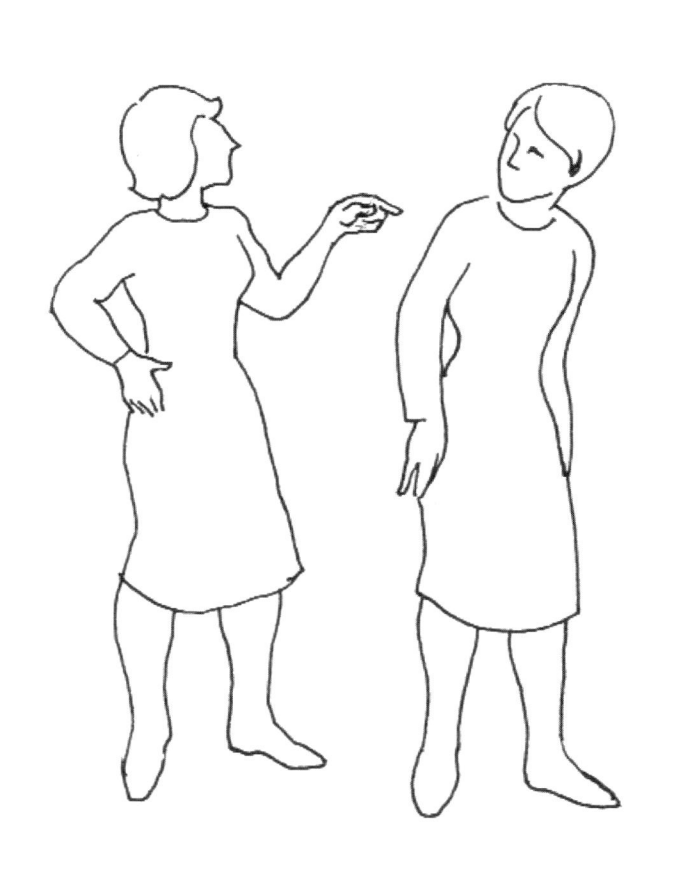

The human game

It seems to me that, in general, human beings take themselves far too seriously. Life on Earth is full of challenges, yes, or it wouldn't be of any value as a learning experience, but it was never intended to be a vale of tears. Today's crisis is usually gone by the time tomorrow becomes today. How well do you remember the happenings of last week, not to mention last month or last year? The game doesn't matter - it's how you play whatever game you choose that matters.

Trust

If you're in a situation that you find intolerable I suggest that you look at it, determine what it is about it that you find intolerable and then hand it over unconditionally to your guides, divine consciousness, the God within, whichever is most comfortable for you. If you allow yourself to trust in the process with no reservations, no conditions, I promise you that the outcome will be a source of wonder and of joy to you.

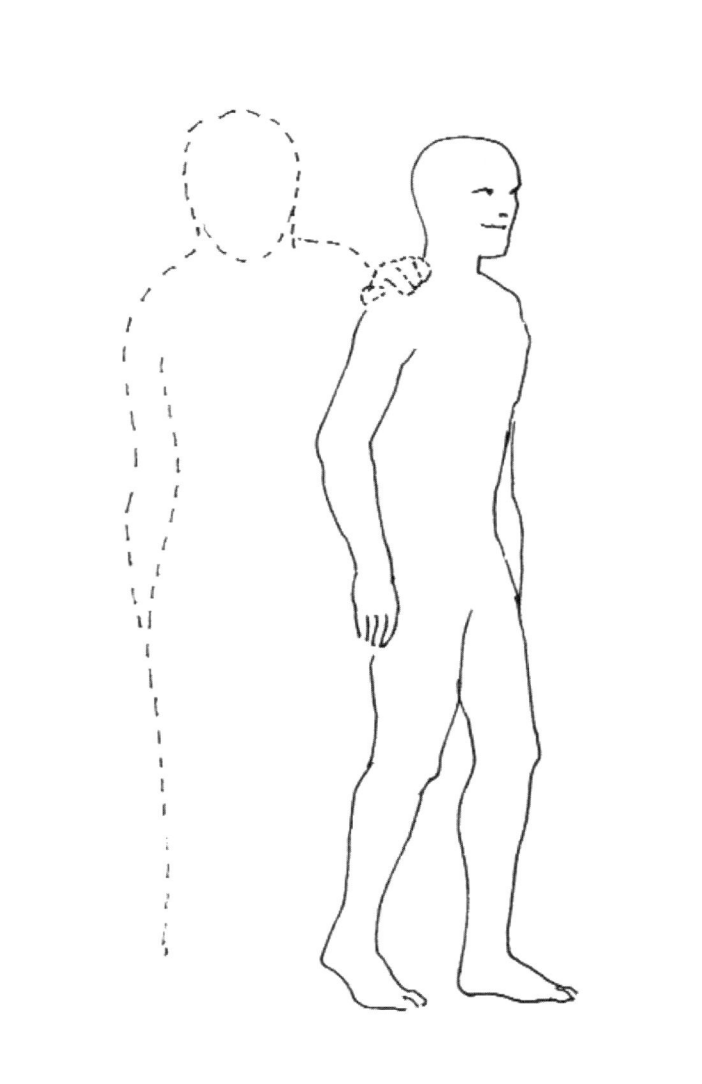

After handing over?

You have handed over unconditionally. What next? You still have to go on living your life. How does the solution happen? You are, of course, a participant in the emergence of a solution. You literally "go with the flow", do whatever feels best to you, constantly reminding yourself of your unconditional handing over of the situation. Life is never stagnant. There's nothing passive about the handing over process. It means aligning yourself with all the evolved energy of the universe in fulfilling your life purpose.

Doing : undoing?

Doing, as commonly understood, is often not doing, or undoing: a reinforcement of negativity. What humans tend to see as reality is a passing parade of events and things and even human existence which are replaced and remembered or forgotten like yesterday or last week or last month or last year. If you don't accept that your reality is internal it's impossible for you to be yourself; you're mainly living your life as a puppet or an automaton. The doing follows automatically and at the best times when the (internal) reality is created and accepted.

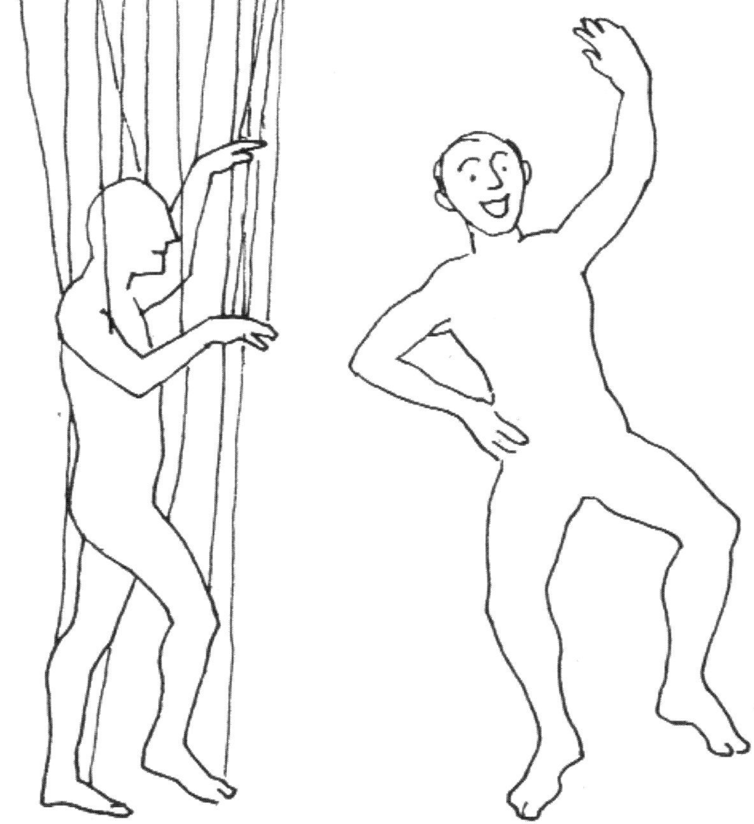

Inspiration

All through history people who have helped to raise awareness have been able to do so because they consciously left themselves open to inspiration. That in no way diminished them; rather the reverse, since they reached out beyond the limits of the physical framework to tap into the universal consciousness. Even though we are each individual, yet we are all one, so that my contribution to the universal consciousness is equally yours as yours in mine. That's why it's so important that each soul finds its way back to full awareness; in doing so it automatically helps every other soul.

Sharing : Influencing

There's a big difference between sharing your thoughts with others and seeking to influence them to your way of thinking. I might have said that there's all the difference in the world but it would be more accurate to say that there's a world of awareness in the difference.

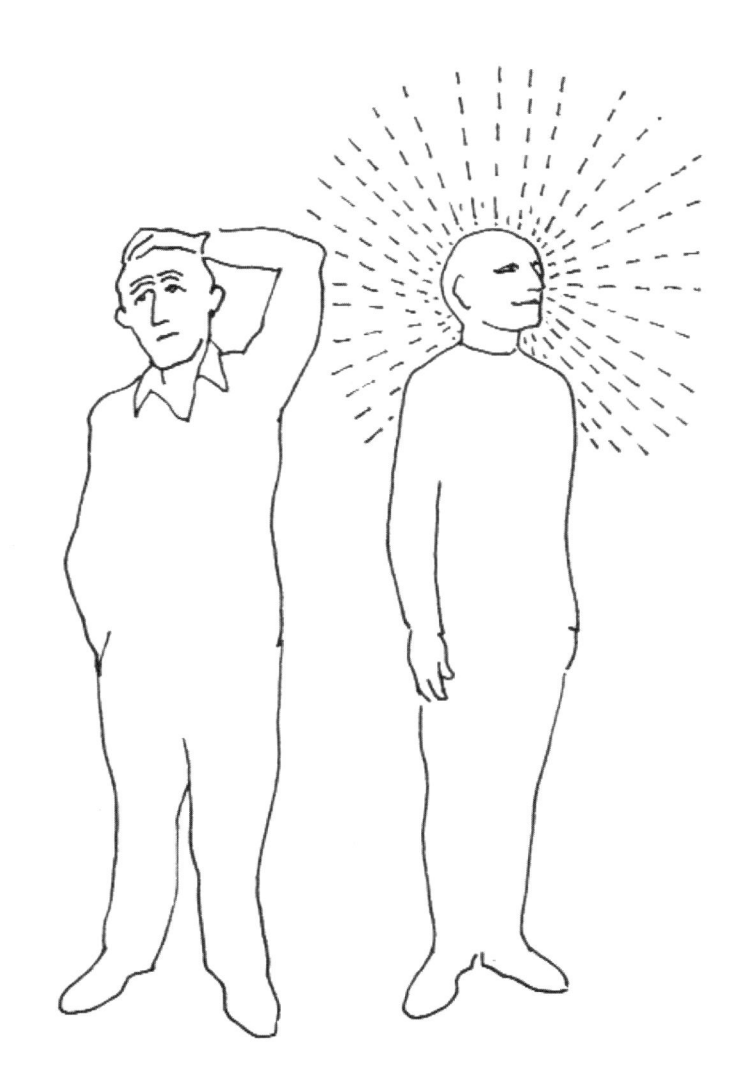

Breaking barriers

What's happening in the present shift in consciousness is that the spirit and physical worlds are being moved closer together. It's much easier now to envisage a time when the barriers between the worlds will be broken down completely, as they are partially at present, and continuing communication will be possible (although maybe not always desired!) between souls in physical bodies and those who have left the physical scene.

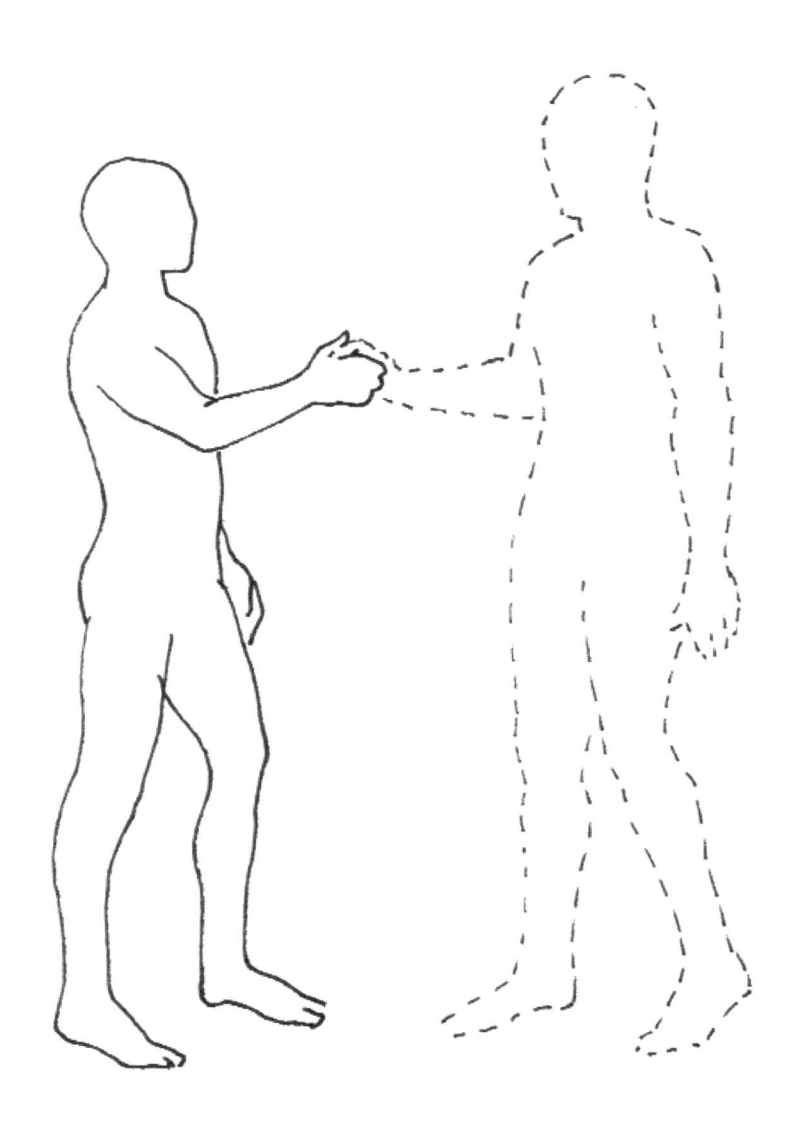

Finding yourself

My approach is basically uncomplicated; if there's a choice between a simple and a difficult way of achieving the same result, choose the simple way. If you have luggage to carry, it's much easier to let it be carried for you by whatever mechanical means are available to you than to carry it on your back. Your guides will help to relieve you of the burden of unawareness if you allow them to do so. Then you will find yourself sooner. It's always nice to find something you lost, isn't it? - not to mention something as valuable as yourself!

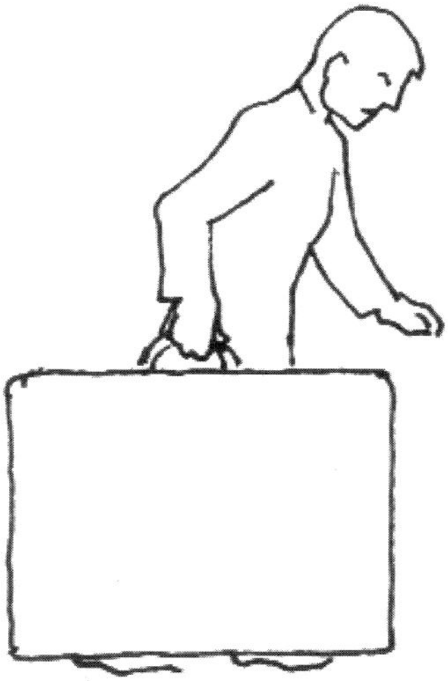

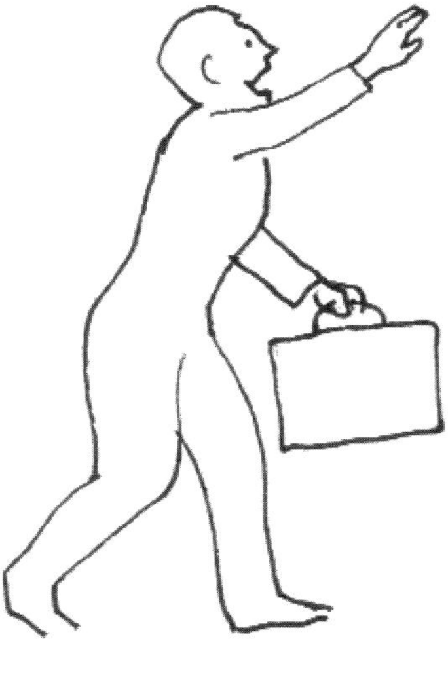

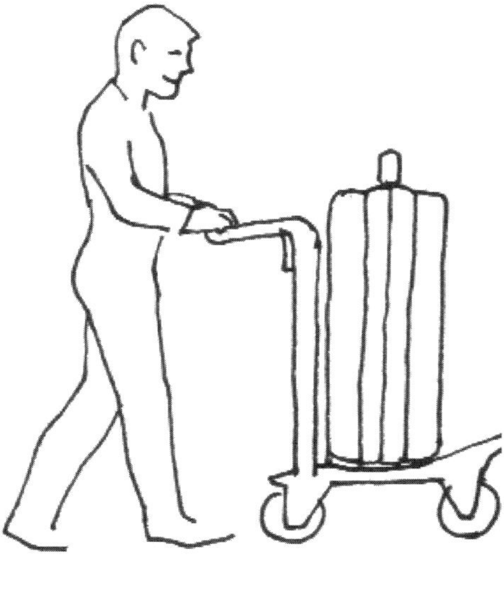

Growth in awareness

As their awareness grows, or more accurately, as their unawareness diminishes, spiritual travellers will be more and more conscious that they have access to all the evolved energy of the universe but that that consciousness does not give them any right to set themselves above others or to exert dominion over them. Accordingly, they will not seek to set themselves up as gurus, or cult figures.

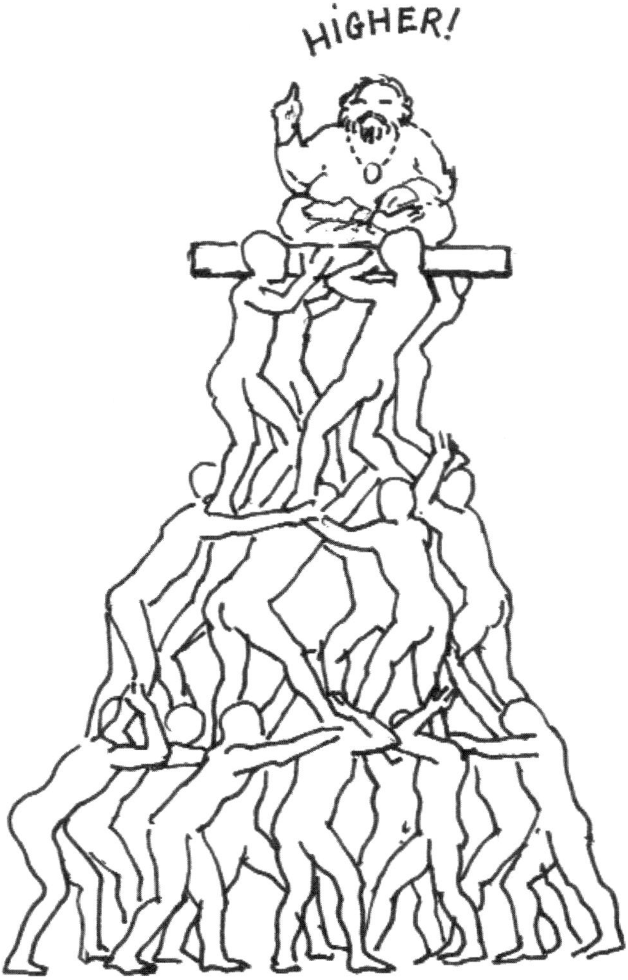
HIGHER!

Happiness

Even though you've forgotten the details you and every other human being and every soul with any awareness know that there's an ultimate happiness waiting for you if you can but find it. The only trouble is that you tend to seek it everywhere but within yourselves which is the only place it can be found in a coming home to the full awareness of your place in God.

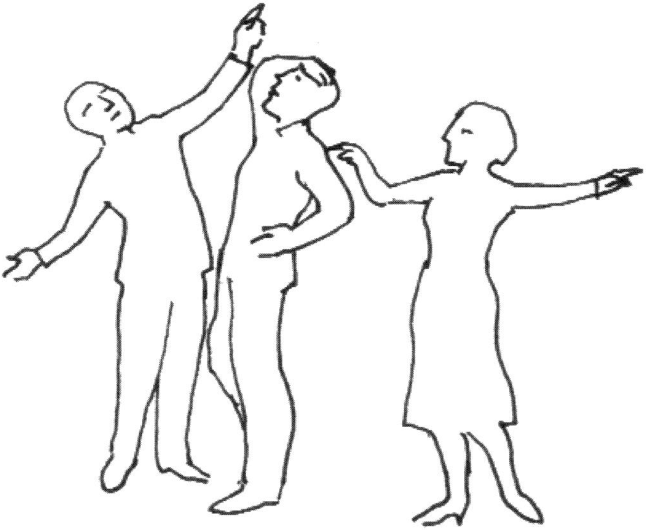

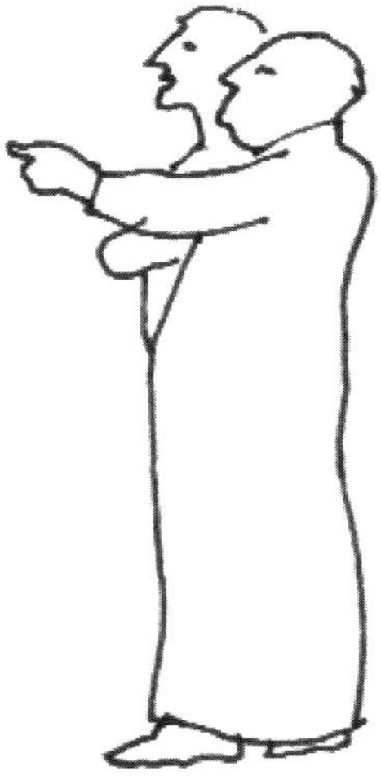

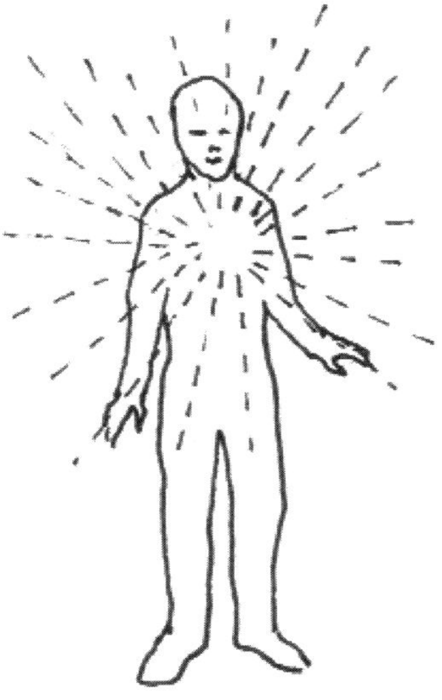

No judgements

The aware soul makes no judgements, moral or otherwise, in relation to others. Your guides are not there to inhibit your enjoyment of life or to condemn you if you, say, drink more alcohol than you can soberly hold. (Your body will probably condemn you enough!) Only you yourself by your own attitude can separate yourself from the joy of spirit (as distinct from spirits!).

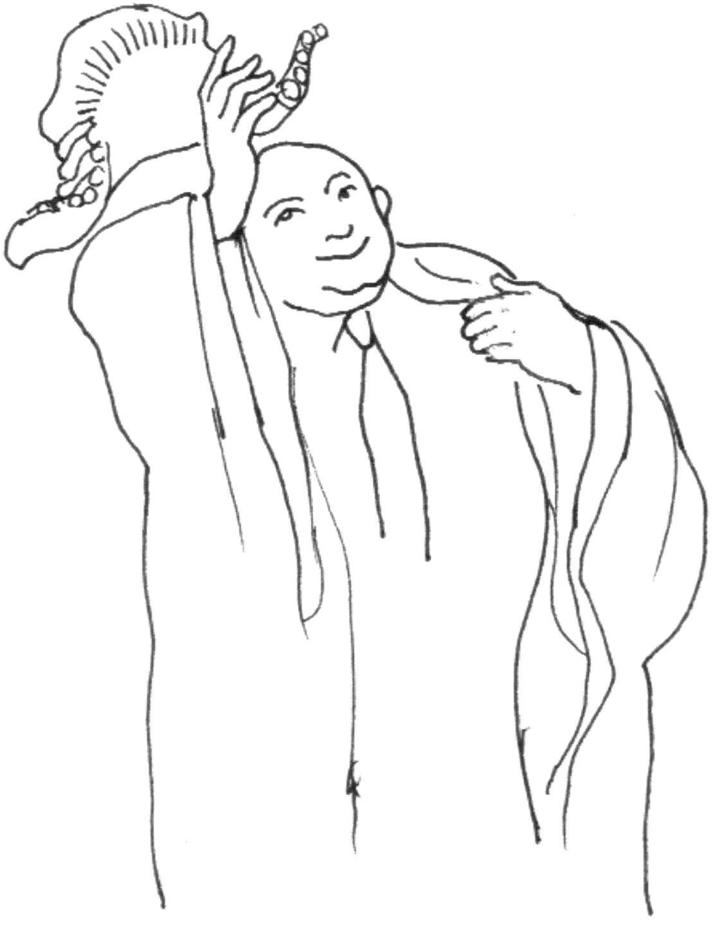

Uniqueness

Please enjoy the wonder of being unique and yet always linked to the loving energy (God) that animates the whole universe. How could you ever be yourself if you had to live eternally within a prescribed set of rules? What could be more marvellous than that you have in store for you the freedom of the universe, with nobody to say to you that you shouldn't be this or do that, that however you are and in whatever way you want to express yourself is entirely a matter for yourself and that you can share yourself and your joy in life with whomever you wish.

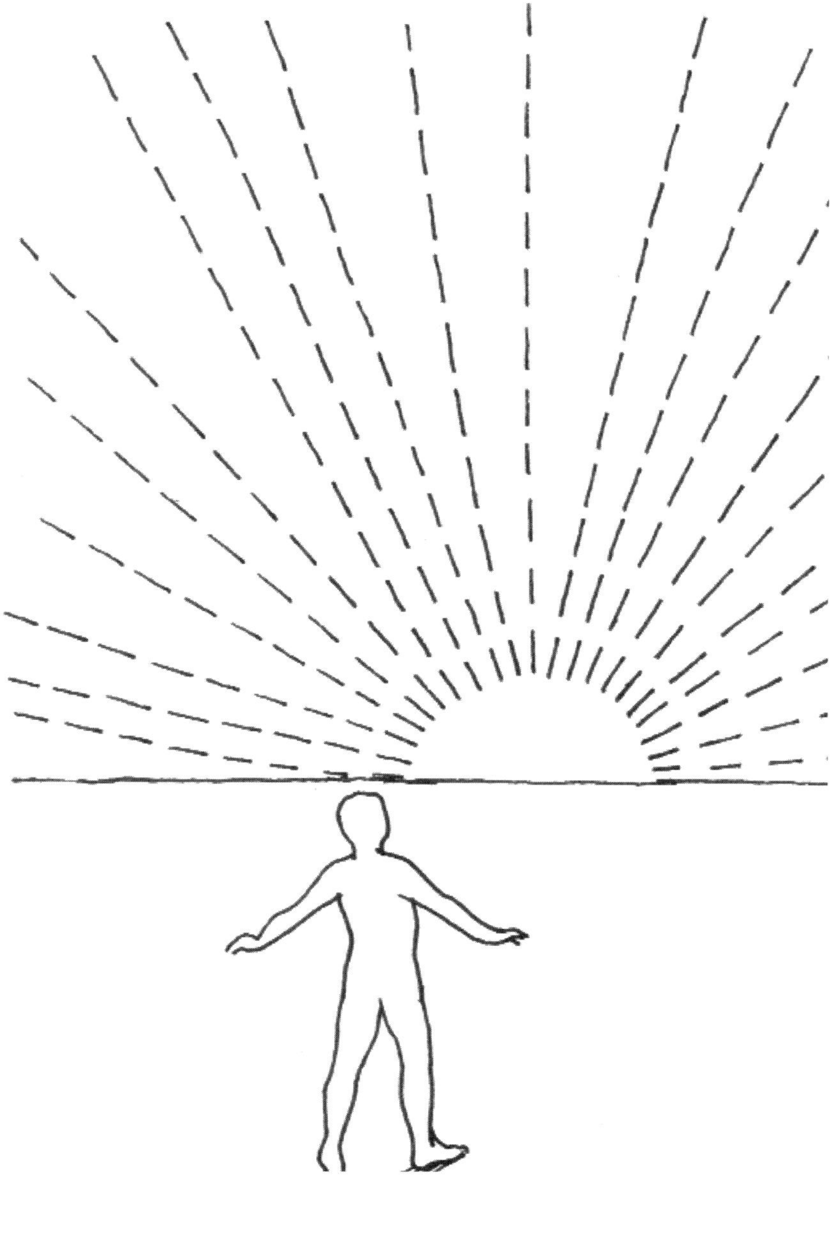

The free spirit

You feel all the burdens, the suffering, the guilt, the weariness, the isolation, the sorrow of humanity lifted from you. You feel your love flowing from you towards yourself, towards all those you hold dear to you and towards all souls; and you forgive yourself for all that followed from your act of separation from your own divinity. All the doubts fade away, there are no more questions to be asked, there's just the ineffable
joy of being.

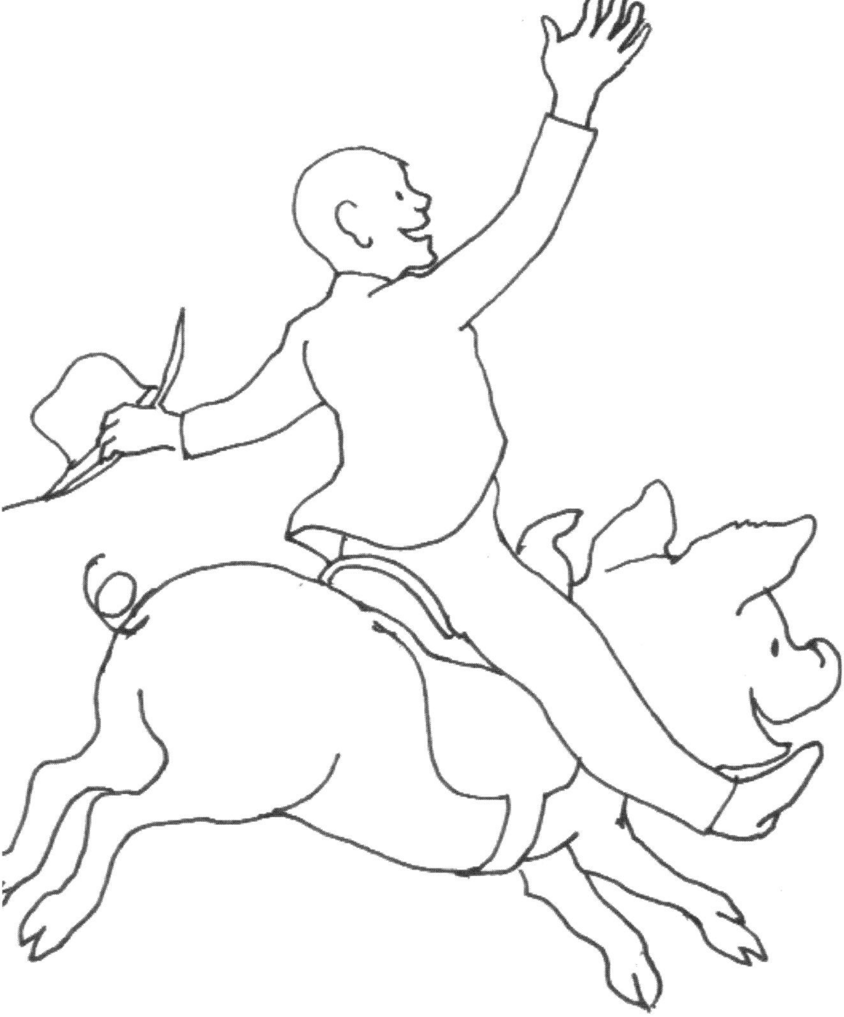

EXTRACTS
from some reviews
of *The Grand Design* series

❄ ❄ ❄ ❄ ❄ ❄ ❄ ❄

"If you are seeking wisdom, you have found it in this book"
Kindred Spirit (Vol I)

" . . . . I very much enjoyed this book. Divided into short, easily-digested chapters . . . . the material offered is at once simple, profound and beautifully expressed"
The Greater World Newsletter (Vol I)

" . . . . help is given in finding answers to age-old questions, who or what are we? From whence do we come? What happens when we die? And what is the meaning of our lives?"
Two Worlds, Here and There (Vol I)

" . . . . I totally agree with the blurb at the back of the book 'Pick this book up and read any part of it and you will be spellbound by its beauty and truth' "
The Greater World Newsletter (Vol II)

" . . . . This is down-to-Earth wisdom, coming from a non-judgmental, loving space"
Nexus (all volumes)

" . . . . Collected in these volumes are Shebaka's insights into the God force, the different stages of evolutionary growth, aspects of the physical, mental, and emotional bodies, natural and supernatural phenomena, and the experiences of death and reincarnation. A central theme in the discourses is that 'we are all spirit beings who happen to be on a human journey for a little while' . . . . . These are provocative books that will stimulate thought, discussion - and perhaps even change"
Napra Review (all volumes)

" . . . . *The Grand Design* aims to celebrate the existence of an infinite, all comprehending, cooperative chain of love linking all souls together. . . . . essential reading for readers seeking to understand why they chose a life on Earth and how they can fulfill their life's purpose, while bringing the joy of spirituality into consciousness . . . . readers will find they refer to [the]volumes repeatedly for loving guidance and wisdom".
The Midwest Book Review (all volumes)

" . . . . The subjects dealt with in the books are not previously unheard of and have appeared, in a variety of forms, throughout many works of literature and film. Parallels can be drawn to the US bestseller *The Seat of the Soul* by Gary Sukav. Although the latter book has reached a massive audience here (thanks, in part, to Oprah Winfrey espousing its value), *The Grand Design* maintains a degree of clarity and comprehensiveness superseding that of any American offering thus far"
Irish Voice (all volumes)